IRISH

YOU A MERRY CHRISTMAS

The many moods of Celtic Christmas
arranged for solo guitar

by Doug Esmond

ISBN 978-1-57424-259-1
SAN 683-8022

Cover by James Creative Group

CENTERSTREAM®

"May the road rise to meet you, May the wind be always at your back, May the sun shine warm upon your face, The rains fall soft upon your fields, And until we meet again, May God hold you In the palm of his hand."

Table of Contents
and C.D. Track List

Biography

James Douglas Esmond started playing the guitar in his teens. He received his Bachelor's of Music Theory and Classical Guitar performance from Ithaca College, Ithaca, N.Y. Upon graduating he became involved in church music. He has held positions in various churches, as a guitarist, organist, singer and conductor. In addition to his church work, he also teaches Guitar and Piano at Blue Sky Studios in Delmar, N.Y., and writes and arranges compositions in various genres and styles. He currently serves as the Organist/Music Coordinator at Newtonville Methodist Church in Loudonville, N.Y. He resides in Albany N.Y. with his wife Meighan. You can visit him on the web at : jdesmondmusic.com.

Foreword.

I find Celtic music to be a beautiful mix of simple yet enchanting melodies and delicate ornamentation as well as full of raw power, like the mix of Harp and Bagpipes. The Guitar can of course imitate the former very well, performing delicate music as well as any other, but needs some assistance if trying to evoke the essence of the latter. To aid with creating this sound I chose some different tunings for several of the pieces with would allow for easier fingerings and more sustainability with bass lines, etc. In addition to some wonderful Celtic traditions for the season I have taken several standard favorites, both sacred and secular, and arranged in a Celtic, and usually more upbeat style. Both Steel and Nylon string Guitars will be great instruments for playing this music and I have recorded using each for half of the pieces. This is music which is wonderful if played solo but could also easily be added to with other instruments and some examples of this are heard on the CD as well. So whether enjoying them by yourself or in the company of other musicians and friends have a wonderful time and a merry Celtic Christmas!

Silent Night

Franz Gruber
Arr. by J.Douglas Esmond

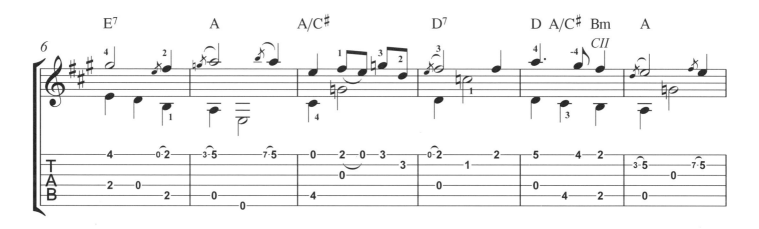

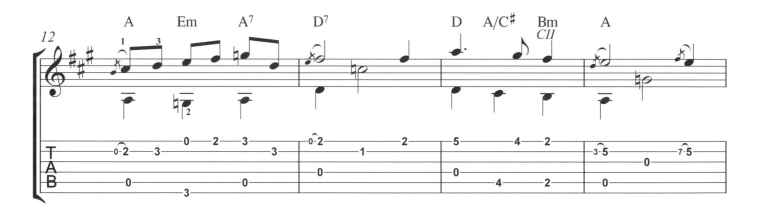

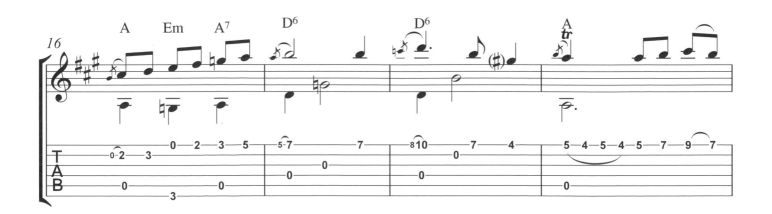

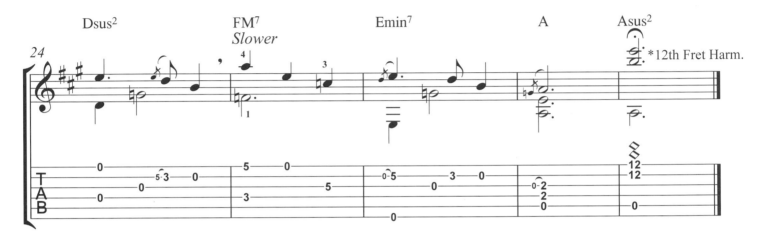

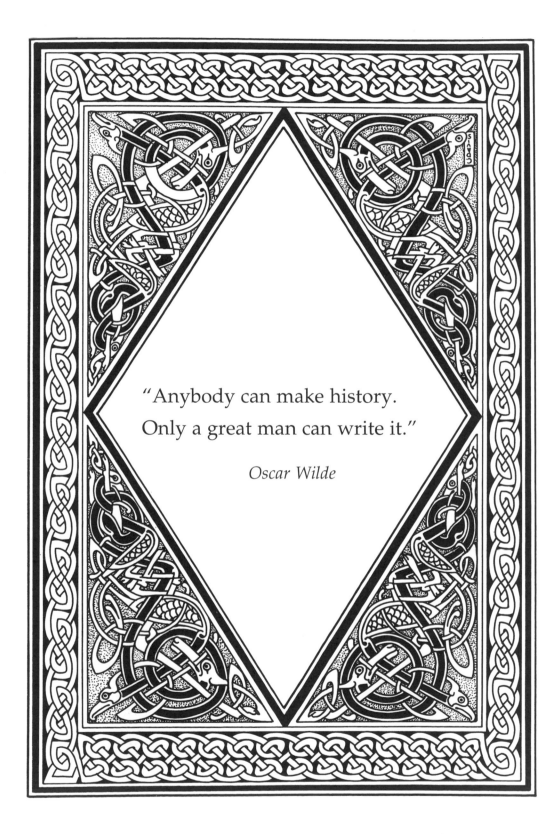

"Anybody can make history.
Only a great man can write it."

Oscar Wilde

My Darling Asleep

Tuning : D,A,D,G,B,E

Traditional Irish
Arr. by J.Douglas Esmond

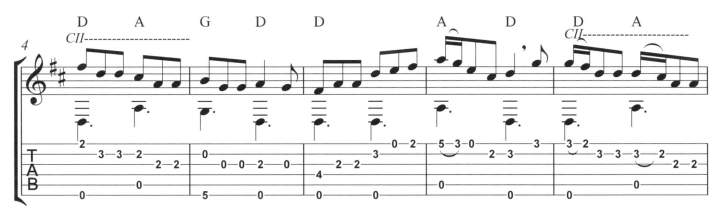

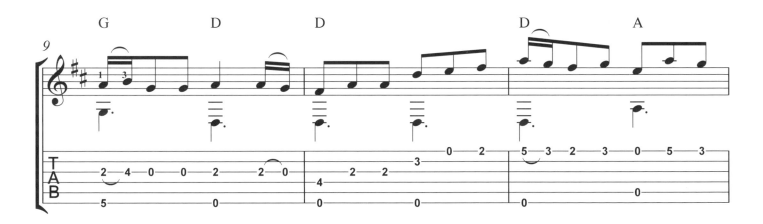

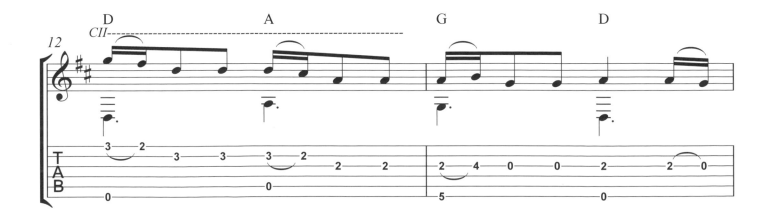

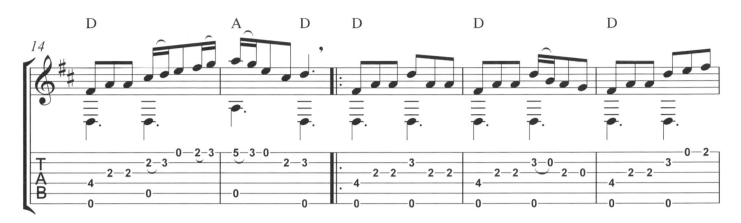

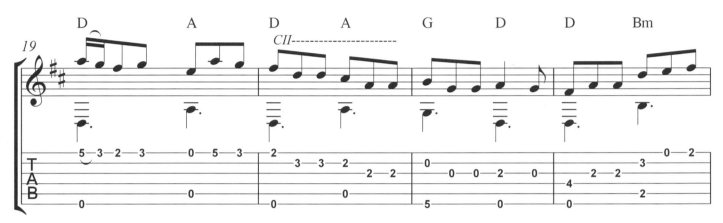

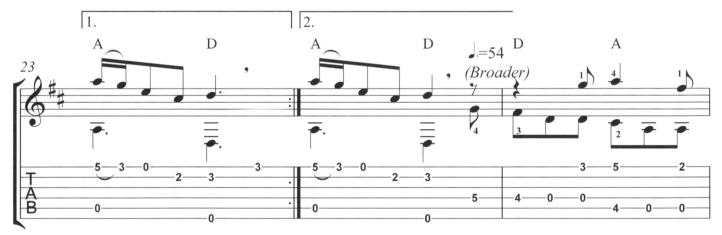

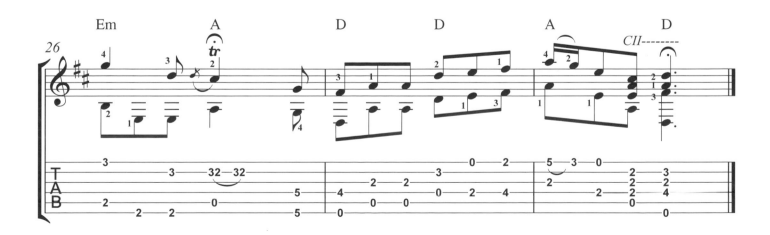

What Child Is This?

Tuning : Standard

Traditional
Arr. by J.Douglas Esmond

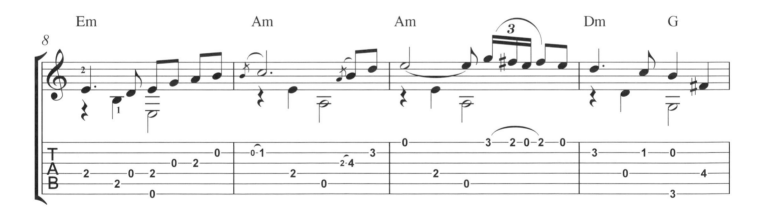

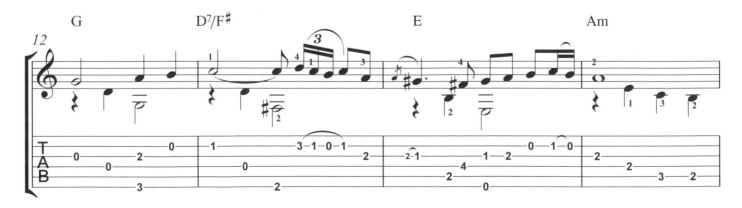

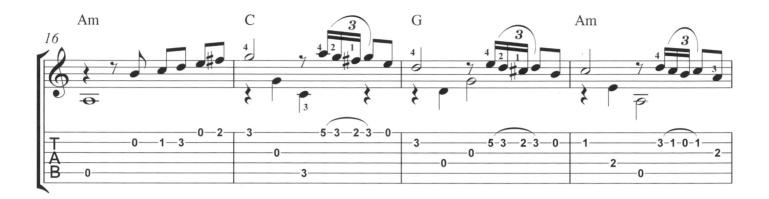

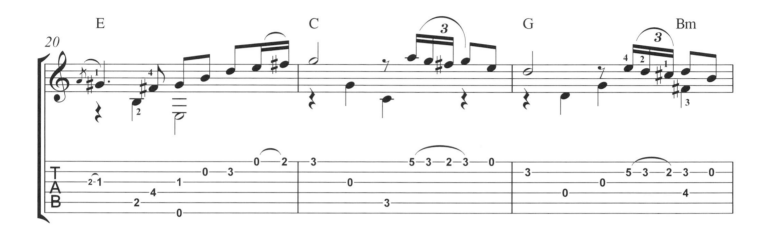

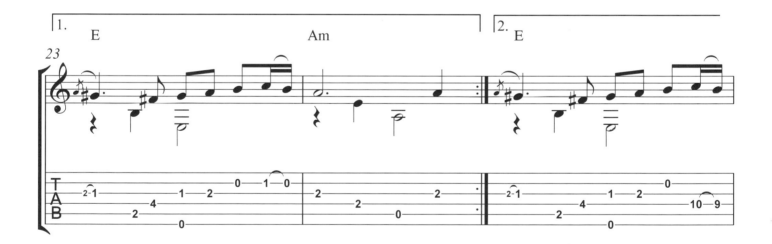

13

The Seven Joys Of Mary

Tuning : Standard

Traditional Irish
Arr. by J.Douglas Esmond

Joyful and Light

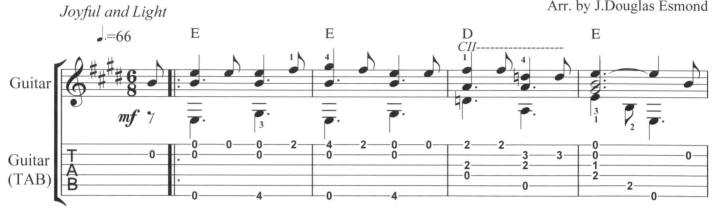

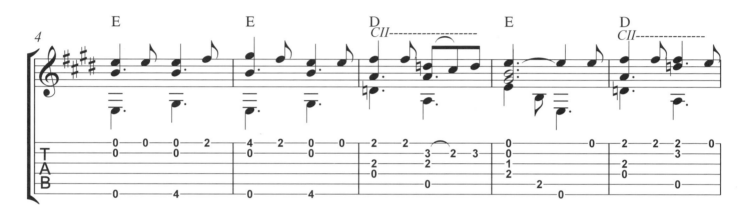

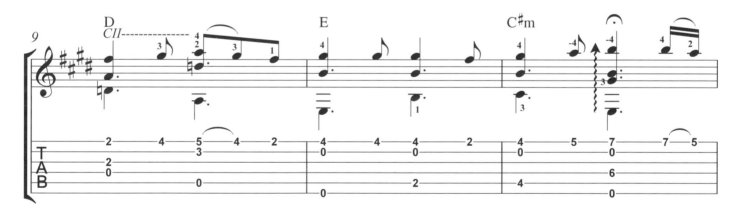

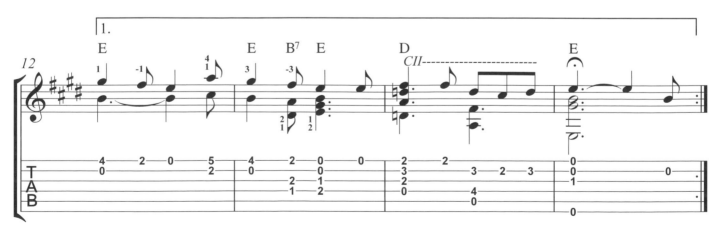

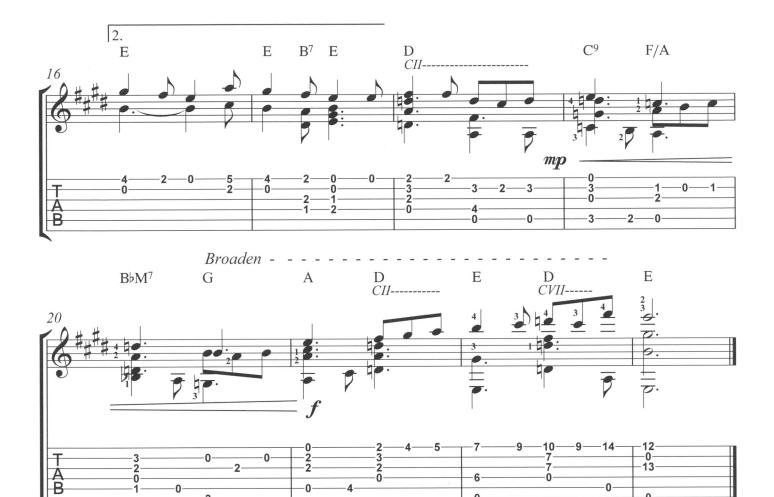

I Saw Three Ships

Tuning : Standard

Traditional
Arr. by J.Douglas Esmond

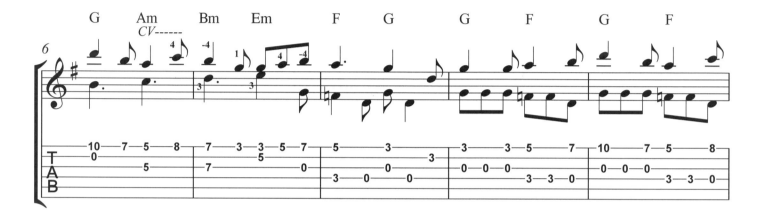

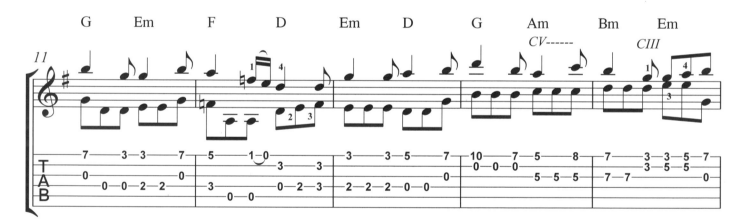

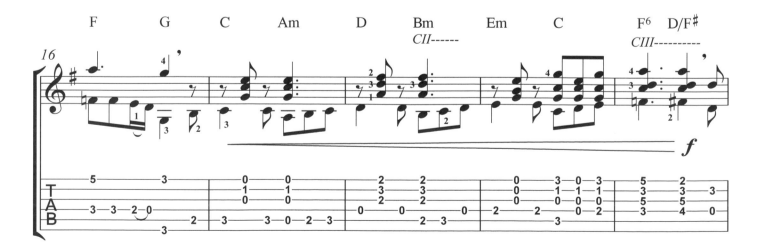

16

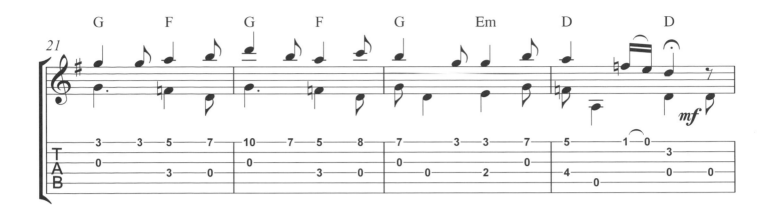

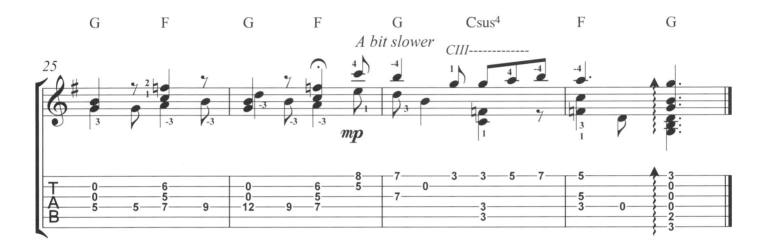

Celtic Cradle Song

Tuning : E,G,D,G,B,E

Traditional Scottish
Arr. by J.Douglas Esmond

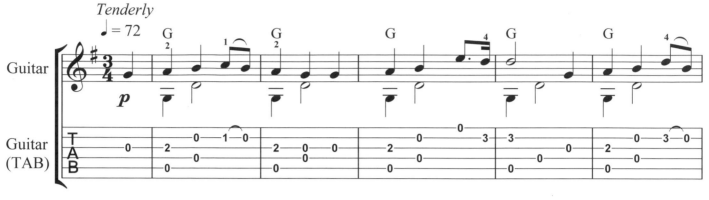

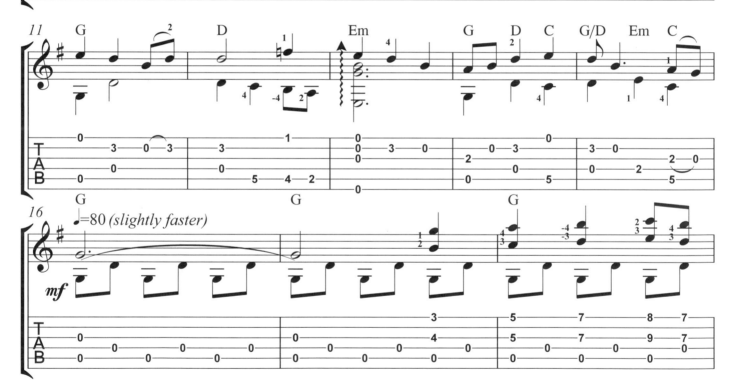

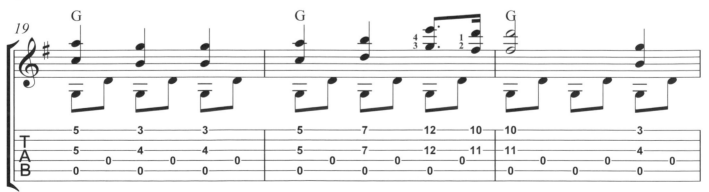

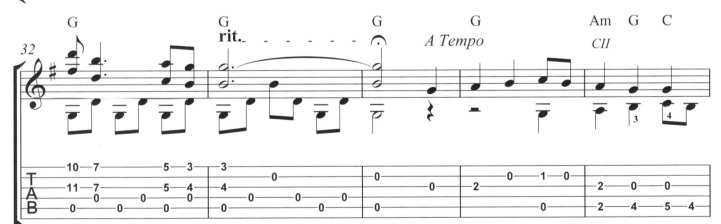

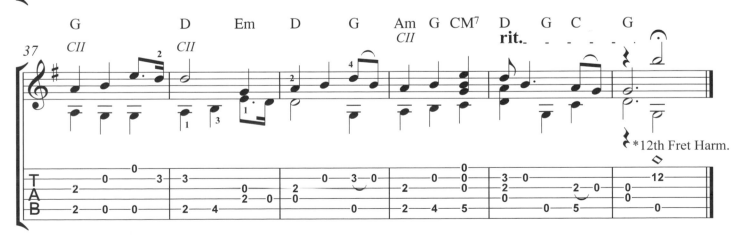

We Wish You A Merry Christmas!

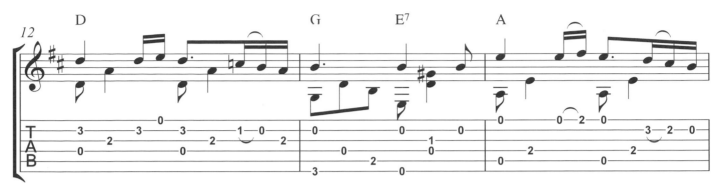

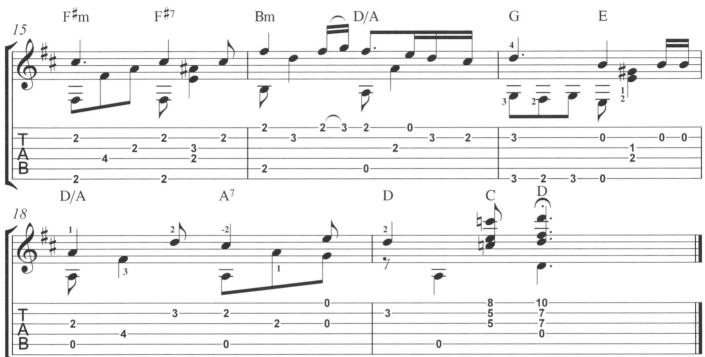

Come Fill Up Your Glasses

Tuning : Standard

Traditional Irish
Arr. by J.Douglas Esmond

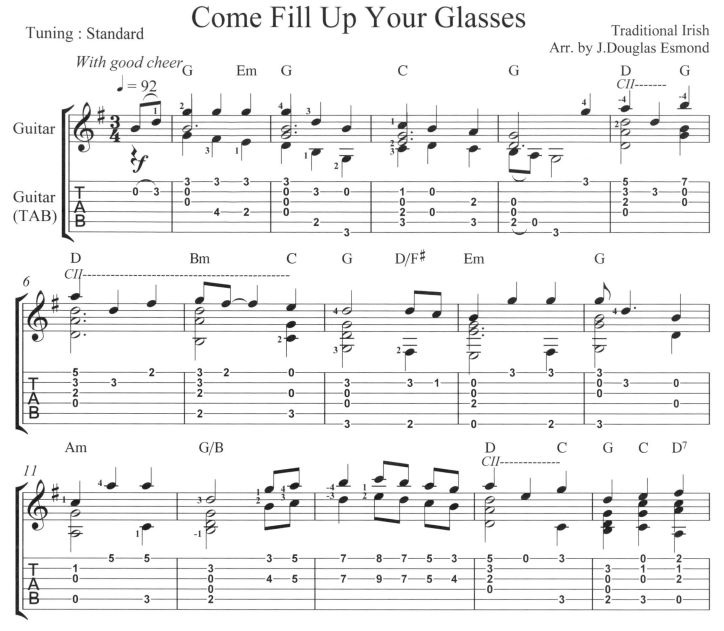

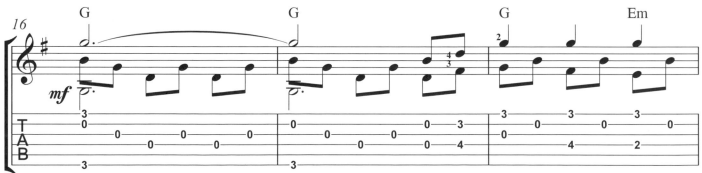

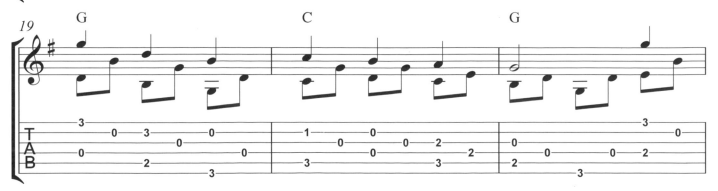

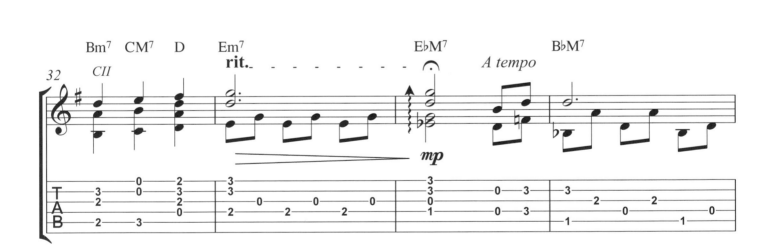

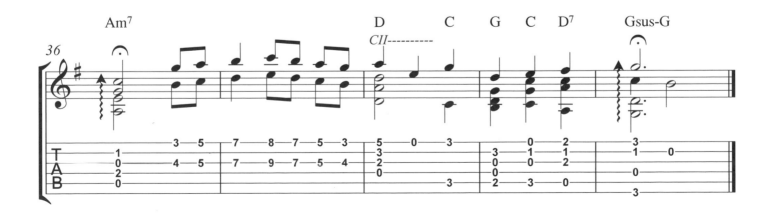

Gloomy Winter

Tuning : Standard

Traditional Irish
Arr. by J.Douglas Esmond

*continue rolling chords

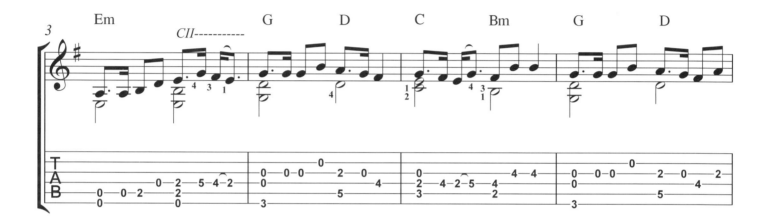

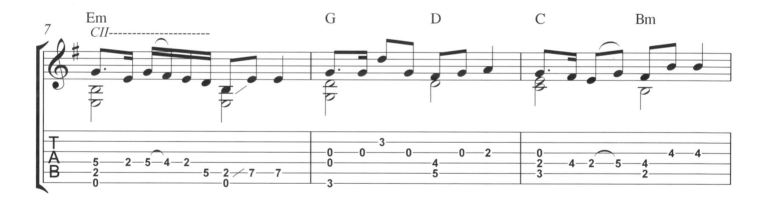

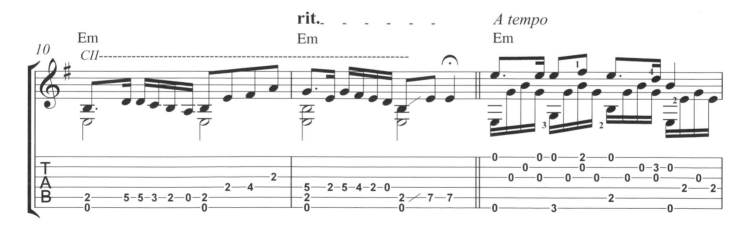

24

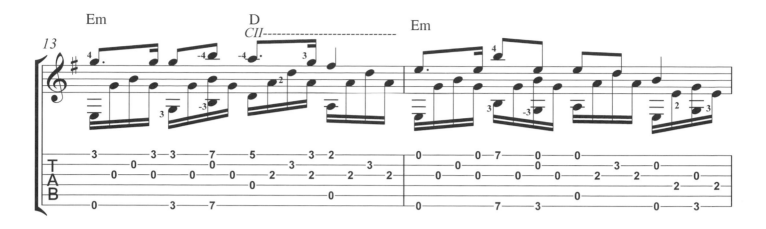

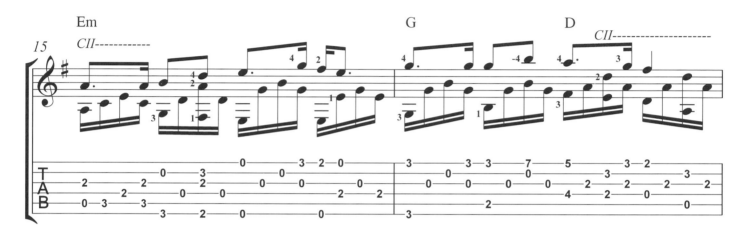

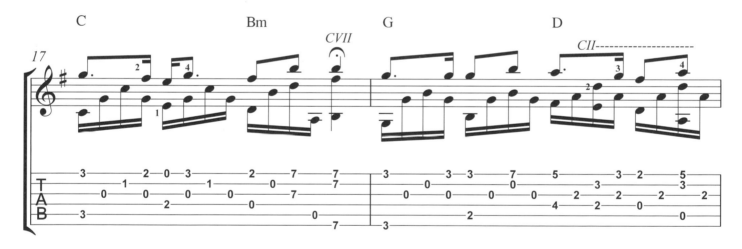

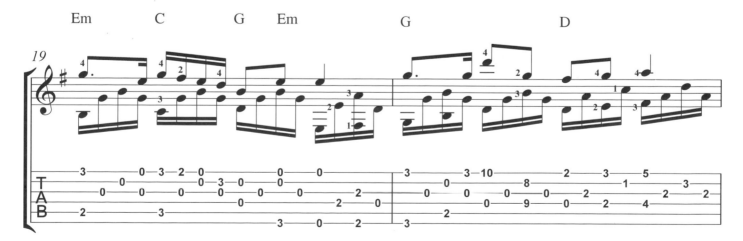

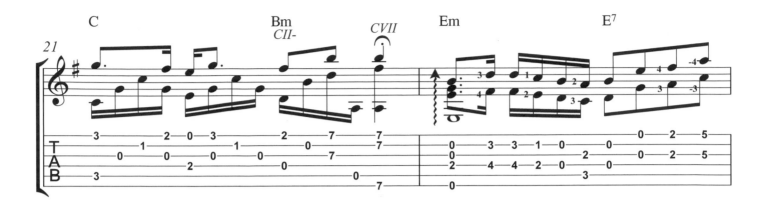

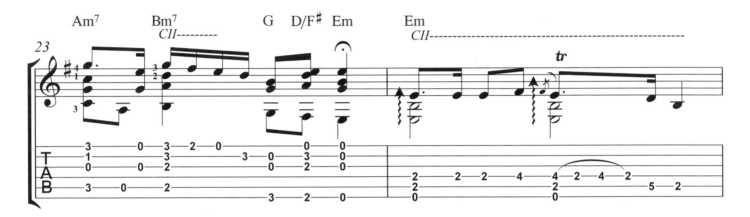

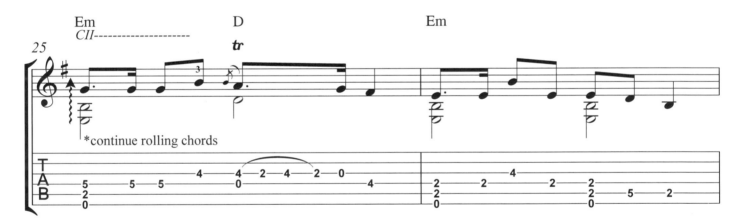

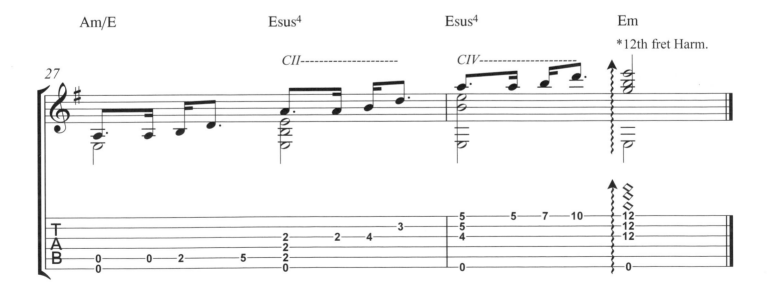

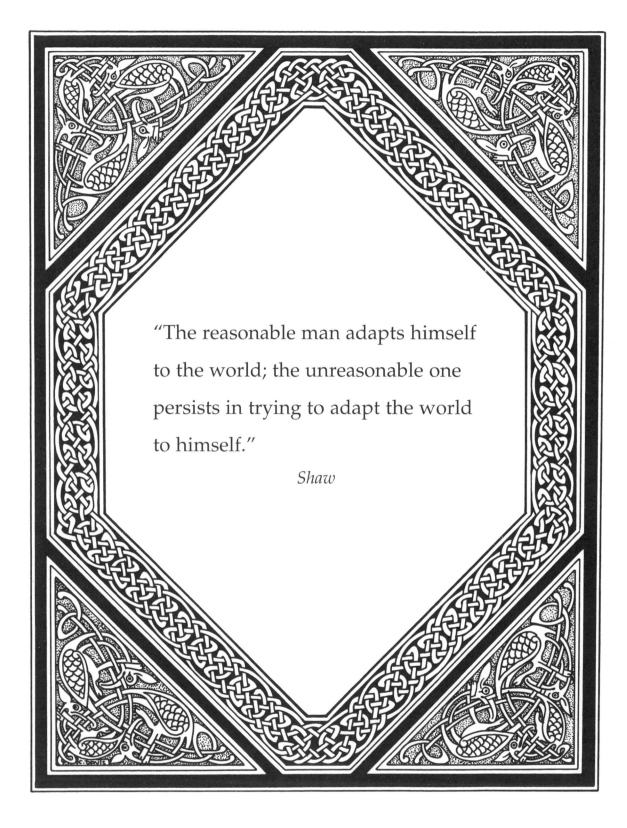

"The reasonable man adapts himself
to the world; the unreasonable one
persists in trying to adapt the world
to himself."

Shaw

O Come All Ye Faithful

Tuning : E,G,D,G,B,E

Traditional
Arr. by J.Douglas Esmond

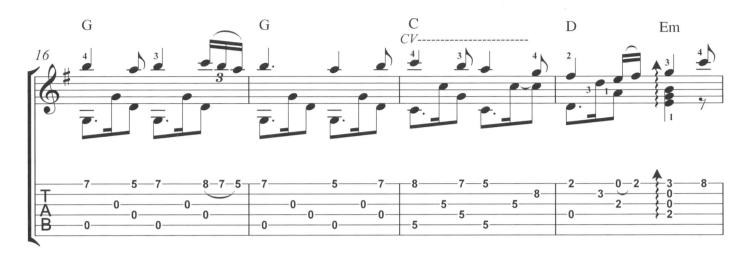

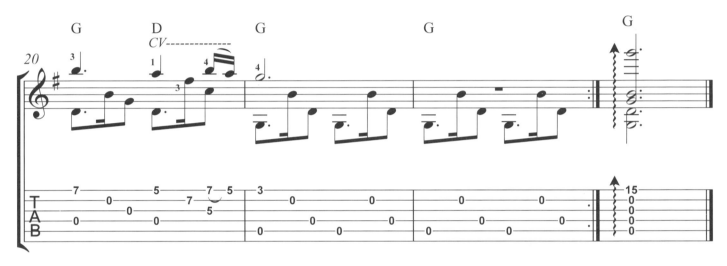

Auld Lang Syne

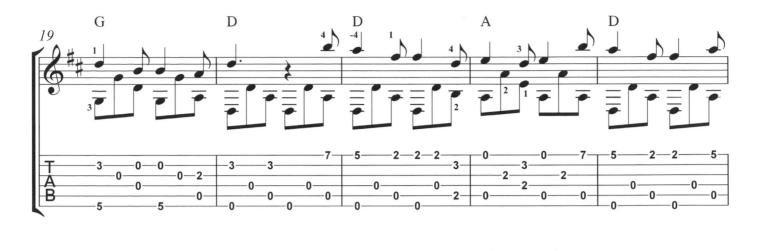

Broadening, calmer

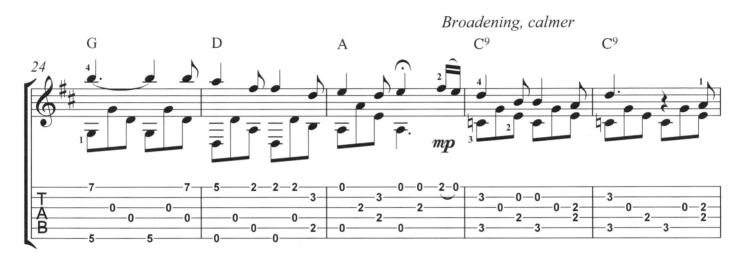

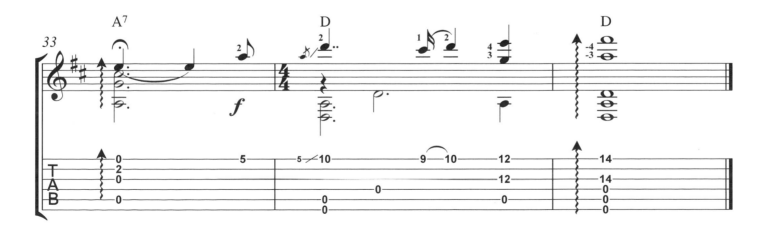

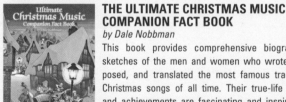